The Less Said, the Truer

The Less Said, the Truer

New and Selected Poems, 2016–2022

Samuel Hazo

Syracuse University Press

Some of these poems have appeared in *Modern Age*, *Notre Dame Magazine*, *Literary Matters*, *Angelus*, the *Pittsburgh Post-Gazette*, *Pittsburgh Quarterly*, *Golden Laurel Anthology*, *Commonweal*, *Dappled Things*, *Capitol Hill Citizen*, and *The Yale Review*.

Other poems in this book were drawn from three previously published books: *They Rule the World* (Syracuse University Press, 2016), *When Not Yet Is Now* (Franciscan University Press, 2019) and *The Next Time We Saw Paris* (Wiseblood Books, 2020). Grateful acknowledgement is made to all three presses for permission to reprint selected poems from these three books in *The Less Said, the Truer*.

First Edition 2022

22 23 24 25 26 27   6 5 4 3 2 1

∞ The paper used in this publication meets the minimum requirements
of the American National Standard for Information Sciences—Permanence
of Paper for Printed Library Materials, ANSI Z39.48-1992.

For a listing of books published and distributed by Syracuse University Press,
visit https://press.syr.edu/.

ISBN: 978-0-8156-3789-9 (hardcover)
978-0-8156-1152-3 (paperback)
978-0-8156-5575-6 (e-book)

Library of Congress Cataloging-in-Publication Data
Names: Hazo, Samuel, 1928– author.
Title: The less said, the truer : new and selected poems, 2016–2022 / Samuel Hazo.
Description: First edition. | Syracuse, New York : Syracuse University Press, 2022.
Identifiers: LCCN 2022027722 (print) | LCCN 2022027723 (ebook) |
    ISBN 9780815637899 (hardcover) | ISBN 9780815611523 (paperback) |
    ISBN 9780815655756 (ebook)
Subjects: LCGFT: Poetry.
Classification: LCC PS3515.A9877 L47 2022 (print) | LCC PS3515.A9877 (ebook) |
    DDC 811/.54—dc23/eng/20220721
LC record available at https://lccn.loc.gov/2022027722
LC ebook record available at https://lccn.loc.gov/2022027723

Manufactured in the United States of America

To Ken and Betty Woodward

Contents

The Less Said, the Truer

The Less Said, the Truer

> Love comes to men through the eye; to women,
> through the ear.
>
> —Arab proverb

When Cyrano proclaimed his passion
    for Roxanne, he spoke from the shadows.
Seated on her balcony, she never
    even saw the man but loved
    what she heard.
                            There's more
    to this than mere romance.
All those who say that love
    is based on age, height,
    religion, status, wealth or race
    are talking mergers, not marriage.
The man a thoughtful woman
    allows to enter her body
    needs more than these to qualify.
It's what she hears or sees
    in his eyes that matters to her.
For lack of an alternative,
    call it the language of the heart.
Bill's wife-to-be spoke only
    Japanese.
                    He felt what she meant,
    and their thirty years together
    prove it.
            Taller than Faisal
    by half a foot, Nouha
    left Syria to marry him

because she liked "the look
in his eye."
        When Anne met
Pamela's French fiancé,
she told her, "I'd marry him
if I had to live in a sewer."
Although her mother disapproved,
    Rebecca explained, "I'm not
marrying my mother."
                Twenty
happy anniversaries later,
she pleaded with guests, "Please,
be nice to my mother."
                What else
but love explains why Trish
mounted a Harley-Davidson
with Mark, who steered it
after midnight through the rain
from Pittsburgh to Washington
with just one stop?
                In order
to prevail, love challenges risk.
Deny that at your peril.

PART ONE

Now and at the Hour

Can you be five years gone?
With those who claim that love
    is more than breath in a body,
    I disagree.
               In health or in decline,
    the body and life are one.
Though life in full means union
    and reunion, life's no less
    when balance is unsteady,
    and nothing seems to help,
    and decades vanish.
               Looking
    back and inward mocks looking
    ahead as nothing but a wish.
Some see that wish as hope,
    but hope is not as true
    as touch or driving together
    to Ferney-Voltaire or seeing
    Sam, Dawn, and our three
    grandchildren at lunch . . .
               Losses
    lessen life but deepen gratitude.
I'm grateful now for all
    we did or tried to do.
               I think
    of us.
          I think of you.

Old Photos Never Die

Her photos show us who
    we were before she left us:
Sam at seventeen in a red
T-shirt—Anna smiling
    and ready to solo at fourteen—
Sarah completely Sarah
at nine.
            She who posed us
together as one-in-all
or all-as-one seems nearer
than ever.
            What paints and easels
meant to artists, her Leica
meant to her.
            Last month
I emptied boxes of multiple
copies of group photos.
She'd made enough for everybody
    in each group to have a copy.
It was something she always did
    without being asked or expecting
anyone to thank her.
            One mother
said in tears, "If not for Mary Anne,
how would I ever know what
my children looked like growing up?"

Stone Time

1

Alike through time since Genesis,
    they've simply endured.
                    It eases me
    to touch, notice or walk
    on them.
          Stone walls, churches
    of stone, stone sidewalks . . .
                   Ever
    since their birth at Creation,
    stones last without aging.
              Touch
    any boulder, rock, or pebble
    anywhere, and you're touching
    something as old as the earth.

2

Stone homes appear to be
    assembled, not built.
              To call
    a stone home a stone house
    sounds derogatory.
             With each
    stone fitted in place, a stone
    wall is a puzzle, completed.
Engraved in stone, all names
    seem immortal.

              Stones differ
while bricks rhyme.
                    Salesmen
speak bricks.
              Poets speak stones.

Once upon a Song

MacLeish was halfway right
    to say a poem should not mean
    but be.
            But let's be clear.
Since poems exist as words,
    they cannot help but *mean*
    and *be* at the same time.
It's what all poets feel
    when a poem happens to them
    like a song so haunting
    that it wants to be sung by them
    alone.
           That calls for gratitude,
not pride.
           Robert Frost
    called "poet" a "praise word."
He never said it of himself.
He let his poems say it
    for him.
           When he wrote down
the words, he saw himself
in them the way that eyes
reveal what's seen to the seer.

The Maker's Touch

Alone in your woodshop, you work
    at what's described as carpentry.
For you it's wood art.
                Creating
    sculpture, furniture, or "turnings"
    is how your talent lets
    perfection happen.
             Apart
    from talent, only love
    can do that, but how remains
    a mystery . . .
           Far from perfect
    but perfectible, we all need
    something to make better.
Otherwise, we worsen.
           For some
    it's family, justice, or gardens.
For me it's words and how
    they sound as much as what
    they mean.
         For you it's giving
    wood a resurrected life
    that's handmade and one of a kind.
This lets a rocking chair
    become deservedly authentic
    as a painting or a poem, signed.

          For Edward Palascak

Spoken by Hand

Twenty women were asked
   if they preferred receiving
   written or emailed love letters.
Even if words were the same
   in both, not one chose email.
For them the difference was personal.
Love's not the lone exception.
Authentic signatures on checks
   or contracts guarantee their worth.
Signatures stand for a person
   and seem as true as life
   itself . . .
            For five centuries.
   millions have seen the printed
   name of William Shakespeare.
His only signature survives
   in a letter padlocked in Stratford.
Somehow that name inscribed
   by hand persists to verify
   his legacy.
            It's not a myth.
Handwritten letters or poems
   reassure because they stand
   for what defies dismissal
   by death and death's facsimiles.
Errors in spelling or punctuation
   make them even more personal.

The Unwelcome

A recorded voice tells me
    that the warranty on a car
    I sold five years ago
    has expired.
                  Another says,
    "I'm Crystal with news about
    your HMO."
                    "Can you hear me?"
asks a third voice and claims
    he needs my vote.
                  Someone
    whose "name is unavailable"
    calls me five times a day.
Telephoning trusted friends
    competes with interrupting pitches.
Since speech is what unites us,
    I call disrupting or recorded
    interrupters nothing but liars.
Just listen to them!
                  They lure.
They read from prompters and mock
    the only time we have
    to share the world we know . . .
What passes for writing today
    does just the same.
                  Penmanship
    that links letter with letter
    is on the wane.
                  Instead
    we finger, click, and shift.

Result?

Typewritten print . . .
But writing what we feel
at pen point seems sacred
as breath.

It says what lovers
say in whispers.

Nothing's more
intimate.

Nothing lasts longer.

The Face We Face

It all began with a myth.
The surface of a pool reflected
    Narcissus to Narcissus
    so handsomely that he fell
    in love with himself.
                   The age
of mirrors followed.
                 And then,
photography.
              Before photography,
the visual past was memory—
just memory.
              Photography
revived the dead—the lost—
the unforgettable.
              Each
yesterday returned as today
forever.
          The problem was
photography's frankness.
                Photos
that pleased were kept in albums
or frames while the rest were
junked.
         Narcissus convinced
everyone but Bill Stafford.
For his book jackets Bill picked
    unflattering headshots as if
    to stress that words outrank
    the chosen deception of faces.

A Picture's Worth a Thousand

Though onlookers look
    different than onlookers
    being looked at, in photographs
    we all look looked at.
A century or so back,
    all people being photographed
    looked the same: groomed,
    seated, and stern.
                       When the same
    people learned that cameras
    could be friendly, everything
    changed.
              Smiles happened.
Posing happened.
              Looking
    looked at meant wanting
    to be seen not as you looked
    but as you thought you looked . . .
We act the same when all
    that needs renaming is renamed
    as we prefer.
              Whether accepted
    or denied, it makes us think
    that what is grudgingly true
    of goodness, malice, or chance
    looks truer and better falsified.

The Surprise

1

Arriving unforeseen and unexpectedly
    as love, they never take no
    for an answer.
                None who
    live by rules or clocks
    can know how poems-in-waiting
    happen.
            Poets themselves
    cannot explain it.
                Inspired,
    they feel obsessed and chosen.
    Afterward, they realize
    they had no option but compliance.
They had to wait for words
    to come to them until
    they saw that writing and waiting
    to write were one and the same.
When a poem decides to start,
    it starts.
            When a poem decides
    it's time to stop, it stops.

2

All you can do is learn
    to write without illusions
    until the words sing off the page.
When nouns and verbs make music,

something surprising is happening.
You'll wait as long as possible
    for what's evolving into song
    so you can be the singer.
The words that come may be
    a mix of yours and others.
This means you have a lot
    of weeding and whittling to do.
What you retain will be
    destined for readers in a future
    you will never see.
                    Because
    poems have birthdays but no
    funerals, they outlive their authors.
Any poem you write could have
    a fate like that, although
    that's far from certain in advance . . .
After what you hoped to do
    is done, at least as far
    as being done is possible,
    you'll find yourself unable
    to explain just how you did it.

Jots That Went No Further

As if to stress that time
    means nothing in baseball,
    hitters run the bases
    counterclockwise . . .
                            Left-handed
    violinists are rare . . .
                        Burying
    two bodies in one grave
    is the last economy . . .
                    No
    second or third baseman
    or shortstop is left-handed . . .
                                Egon
    Schiele painted contorted
    nudes spread-eagled to reveal
    their pubic hair combed
    neatly down and parted . . .
Being hanged, electrocuted,
    poisoned, shot, or beheaded
    was deemed more merciful
    than being stoned to death . . .
Robins perch at attention . . .
All flatterers presume
    that everyone is vain enough
    to listen . . .
                        Traveling by car,
    jet, or train amounts to sitting
    still in motion . . .
                        We copulate
    to populate . . .

Waiting
for love to find us (or us,
it) is all that matters.

Maura

A Brooklyn girl, raised
   by uncles after her mother
   died and her father remarried,
   she hoped to be a teaching
   sister of poor children.
Instead, she was chosen
   to introduce collegiate girls
   to poetry.
           She also wrote
   books of poems, which read
   like prayers at play.
              Faith had
   its place, but evangelicals
   bored and annoyed her.
Yelled at by one to listen
   to the voice of Jesus in her,
   she answered, "The Jesus in me
   doesn't talk like that."
               She
   and a friend once counseled
   a student who was six feet
   five inches tall and wore flats
   to appear shorter with men
   her age.
        "Liz," they said,
   "you're not marrying mankind—
   one man will solve your problem."
The man Liz married stood
   six feet and ten inches high.

When a literal lawyer asked Maura
  if she used a Bible in class,
  she said, "I prefer the *New Yorker*."
She rejected administrative posts
  because she believed they destroyed
  friendships.
            When a young mother
  asked if her son could take
  her picture, Maura's blue eyes
  said yes.
            The boy took five
pictures.
            Each one captured
  a fraction of Maura's forehead.
The mother apologized.
            Maura
  kissed the boy and said,
  "What a beautiful sky!"
Retired in her nineties, she sat
  by herself and spoke only
  when needed.
            Her nurses said
  she was waiting for God to call her.
Maura might have added, "He'll
  be unexpected and late as usual,
  but the waiting should be worth it."

Sister Maura Eichner SSND, 1915–2009

The Sum of Us

What is heredity but centuries
   of births, deaths, journeys,
   weddings, wars, surprises,
   and griefs?
           History becomes
   no more than outdated updates
   of dateless orbits of the earth.
In time these turn irrelevant
   or vague as honors and as vain.
Outliving Eden and its myths,
   we find in space what
   saves us.
           Since breath has
   no birthdays, I say that Genesis
   begins all over every time
   we breathe.
           Each time I face
   a mirror, I'm looking at Adam.

A World of Difference

I've outgrown the world.
                    I'm
    overinformed but none
    the wiser.
              Braggarts choose
    with care their personal hells.
Sloganeering with a microphone
    presents itself as oratory.
Art seems random as paint
    splattered on a wall or splashed
    on the floor.
              Cameras film
    performances on beds, beaches,
    or battlefields.
                    Sebastian Maniscalco
    put tattoos in their place with:
    "You don't put bumper stickers
    on a Ferrari."
              Before addressing
    Congress, the ruler of a client
    nation boasted to his staff,
    "Leave these Americans to me."
During his speech the seated
    suckers stood to applaud him
    twenty-seven times.
                    Advertisers
    on television do the same
    each day but slicker.
              Saints
    of the imagination have no voice.

For peace I choose the strength
of least resistance—five minutes
in my favorite porch chair.
The grass seems always greener.
The sky is April blue.
Pigeons strut like the wives
of kings.
A chipmunk chews
his chestnut.
Irises bloom.
It's nothing but live and let live
in the first and undefiled world.

Right of Way

Nothing can match the pink
    of azaleas in total bloom.
Each April they repeat
    themselves on cue.
                The same
    is true of maples—any maple.
Headlines repeat themselves
    but less creatively.
                China
    replaces Russia, which replaced
    Iraq, which replaced Libya,
    which replaced Afghanistan,
    which replaced Vietnam,
    which cannot be replaced.
We Americans prefer priority
    to parity while body counters
    tally what we've lost.
              We did
    just that until a microscopic
    virus claimed more victims
    in a year than all our losses
    since the Revolution.
          This irony
    is wasted on those whose only
    enemies are one another.
              While
    nations vie for primacy
    and power, superiority is
    nature's way to be supreme
    until it's checked.

It's never
a question of malice but measure.
Rendered harmless by injections,
a virus will survive thereafter
within limits.
Respecting
equidistance, every maple
does the same.
Evading
frosts, azaleas in April
will blossom pinker than ever.

No Option but One

Whatever could have been
   or still might be comes
   without warning in our sleep.
The days of pain that never
   happened happen.
             Dreams
   of bounty or misjudgment differ
   only in degree and outcome
   from nausea to guilt.
             Excess
breeds regret.
          Soldiers
rise legless or armless or both
from ranks of identical graves,
accusing, accusing, accusing.
We struggle not to listen.
Titles like Mr. President,
   Your Royal Highness,
   You Holiness, Your Honor,
   Your Grace, or those who hold
   the office of citizen mean nothing.
The bitter truth of nightmares
   comes without our willing it.
Waking wiser or spared,
   we draw each breath in gratitude.

Marie-Claude de Fonscalombe

A white kerchief ribboned
    her loosely combed black hair.
No ring encircled a finger.
Her tanned cheeks revealed
    no trace of rouge or blemish,
    and she walked like a woman
    without weight.
                        Jacques told me
she was Saint-Exupéry's niece.
I asked how he met her.
He said their families were related.
As she approached, she smiled
    at us.
                    Her figure filled
her blouse and slacks with *girl*
completely.
                    When she stood
before us, she spoke in musical
French.
                    To look at anyone
but her was impossible.
                            "Watch,"
said Jacques, "watch when she walks
away."
            "Why?"
                        "Because
she's beautiful coming or going."
Watching her drive off
    alone, I added, "Or gone."

Without Words

Fouled on purpose, he grimaced
   and limped to the free-throw line
   in silence.
               He let the two
foul shots he sank speak
for him . . .
                 After they made love,
they chose to keep their lips
lightly in touch before
returning to themselves . . .
                     He knew
that twenty-six letters stood
for every sound we say.
The more he looked, the more
   he saw there all the plays
of Shakespeare, translations
of both Testaments, and every
curse or whisper ever uttered . . .
Each time he woke from a dream
   too upsetting to sleep with,
   he smoked a conversational cigar . . .
Seeing her son swear
   at his sister, his mother
   just stared at him until
   he apologized and kissed her . . .
Europe's immigrants watched
   and understood Charlie Chaplin
   because he never spoke.

An Oldster's Dissent

Embracing effort, he
   bannisters his struggle
   up the stairs and down.
Walking is hard, working
   is harder, and waking the hardest.
He's told the cure is rest,
   but all that rest foretells
   is further weakening.
In a doctor's office, a nurse
   asks his age and seems
   shocked when he says, "Ninety."
She asks him to name the President
   and if he knows which day
   it is.
         Later the doctor
apologizes and tells him the nurse
is new.
         The oldster says,
"I've had enough and more
than enough of being told
that wellness is all."
               He calls
retirement a myth of ease
that leads to assisted pre-death
and "resting in peace."
              He adds
that death's in everyone's future,
so all that matters is . . . when.
"Not when," the doctor says, "but how."

Madame Tartuffe

She believes that faith and going
   to church are one and the same.
She makes sure that she is seen
   attending.
                What matters most
   to her is rousing the envy
   of her friends by winning the lottery
   or being seated with celebrities.
Her current cause is claiming
   that immigrants are communists.
A century ago, she would have
   called them hunkies, dagoes,
   krauts, or kikes.
                She's either
   totally *for* or totally *against*.
She's averse to discussion
   and speaks only in conclusions.
Living in a time-shared condo
   in Daytona Beach is her answer
   to January.
                Travel on tourist
   ships is her alternative to trips
   by jet, train, or car.
                Hosting
   dinners for honored guests,
   she flatters the hired help
   with praise but never tips.

Readiness Is Not All

1

Problems attack.
　　　　　You have
to be ready whether you're
ready or not.
　　　　　They overwhelm
like love.
　　　　　The blindfolded
baby with arrow and bow
can hit whatever he's not
aiming at.
　　　　　There's no reprieve.
Shock or infiltration
will surprise and infiltrate.
Targeted, expect no option
but reaction.
　　　　　Delay like anybody
cornered by dilemmas.
　　　　　Pause
before you choose.
　　　　　Weigh all
the consequences.
　　　　　Yesterday's
fool could be tomorrow's
hero.
　　　　　Results cannot
be known in advance.
　　　　　Regret
is just as likely as assurance.

2

Attacks as sudden as lightning
  prove there's no protection
  from surprise but luck.
If warned and given time
  to see the worst is likely,
  you weigh the odds.
                  The worst
  could be tornadoes, hurricanes,
  or war.
          Choosing self-deceit
  before such possible catastrophes
  is understandable . . .
                  The world
  remains in motion while
  you mull.
              If nothing happens,
  you survive intact, but havoc
  by chance is merciless.
                  If warnings
  never come, there is no time
  for anything but pain and panic.
Survival depends on luck,
  just luck.
              If lucky, you'll be
  grateful.
              If not, not.

PART TWO

Life after Lapses

He tells his son the news
    he told him yesterday
    as if old news is new.
Asked his age by a nurse,
    he has to pause and count.
Trying to quote the last
    four digits of his "social,"
    he gets as far as three.
He has trouble reading
    his own handwriting and asks
    for a pen he's already holding.
What gladdened him once
    just maddens him now.
                    Only
    when he says exactly how
    and what he feels does he
    assure himself, but briefly.
In travel he feels safe
    but uncertain as someone
    seat-belted in a hijacked plane.

Mixed Metaphors Mixing

My father had a driver's eyes.
He faced all problems as if
    they were intersections . . .
                    A note
    from my dentist reminds me
    that it's time . . .
                Whenever it's dropped,
    a pill or a penny demands
    to be searched for and found . . .
It's rare to meet someone
    from Wyoming . . .
              Photographs
    prophesy the past . . .
           A home
    is a house that's lived in . . .
How many do you know who've read
    the Declaration of Independence . . .
Away with uniforms, salutes,
    orders, ranks, and parades.
They're all a front for weaponry,
    violence, and murder . . .
               Wars
    will end when two nations see
    in advance that devastation
    and defeat await them both . . .
Cornered in any struggle,
    the lone way out is through . . .
Zeros equal nothing,
    but add zeros to any number
    to learn the power of zero . . .

Poetry means expressing
    the impossible as well as possible . . .
If no one can make love
    on the moon, and nothing can grow
    there, why go there?

Upward to Nowhere

Since up is higher than down,
   whatever evokes ascent
   implies supremacy.
                Higher
   or highest equates rank
   with power.
           For upward thinkers
   heaven is always above
   with hell forever below,
   while old divinities still view
   the world from Sinai or Olympus.
Propped in outdated parliaments,
   highnesses rule but stand
   no taller than the ruled.
Such myths prevail, although
   the wise insist that looking
   within and not just up
   or down is where we'll find
   our time and place.
           And I agree.
To those who say sky-high
   is where we'll look at last,
   I send condolences.
         There's nothing
   to be seen up there but space.

Reactions

After completing his formal
   speech on American drama,
   Arthur Miller invited
   questions from the audience.
The first four questioners asked
   about Marilyn Monroe.
Realizing that answering questions
   about her was why he'd been
   invited, he stood and left . . .
Although Christ said, "The kingdom
   of heaven is within you,"
   many Christians still look
   skyward for salvation . . .
Eva Marie Saint rejected
   "naked Hollywood."
                Unwilling
   to be nudely known, she needed
   nothing but her name for notice . . .
Suspending his fellowship in Paris,
   my brother returned home
   for induction in the army.
                 Instead
   he was rejected for having
   size-thirteen flat feet.
Resuming his studies, he finished
   a book that's still considered
   definitive on love as an idea . . .
After Wilma Rudolph
   recovered from polio, she chose
   to be a runner.

Three gold
medals in the Rome Olympics
awaited her.
But no one,
male or female, could run
like Wilma Rudolph.
She sprinted
in strides while other runners
seemed to be running uphill . . .
Until his late teens, one
boy could not speak a word
without stuttering.
Someone
suggested that reading poetry
aloud might remedy that.
It did.
He's recognizable by voice
today as James Earl Jones . . .
Offered an armored car
on his final trip to Dallas,
Kennedy called it an insult
to the presidency.
Two hours
later he was shot for refusing
to be insulted . . .
Some say
that guns make men.
Cowards
believe that.
Dangerous cowards.

Yours

A pair of brown bedroom
     slippers, boxed . . . three idle
     dresses on hangers, sealed
     in cellophane . . . a bracelet chain
     of coins, medals, rings,
     and a miniature Monticello.
Who was it said we live on
     in what we leave behind?
A coat with one dollar in the left
     pocket . . . snow boots propped
     at attention, never worn . . .
     outdated driver's licenses
     with you photographed smiling
     the same in each.
                    Leftovers
     in sudden abundance make
     our empty house emptier.
I sit in your favorite chair
     with the mute walls for company.

Script for a Widower

The life they both became
    vanished with her.
                       Memory
    is no facsimile.
               She
    who completed him is gone.
He's grown less than entire.
At best he feels half present.
Regardless, he knows that love
    persists, persists.
                 Whether
    he'll ever be complete again
    is unforeseen, unless some ruse
    of hope allows the once
    miraculous to happen twice
    exactly as it was.
             The mind
    denies the likelihood.
The body resists, insists.

Julia at Tyre

> When words and melody inspire, the singer
> and musicians and audience unite and
> create the language of feeling at its best.

Like a woman lost in song,
 she sang a lover's poem
 set to music that brought
 three thousand to their feet.
Clapping, they sang back
 to her the song she sang
 to them.

    It made them one
in ways that went beyond
but stayed within them.

      After
the singing ended, they seemed
as lax as lovers after loving—
smiling, satisfied, and grateful.

One but Separable

The tree is spliced so that
   it blossoms pink on the lower
   branches but white from there
upward.
           Each April this splicing
   of two trunks grafted
   together works to perfection
   with both the newer for it.
It makes me think of twins
   conjoined at birth, then split
   by surgeons but somehow still
   bonded in a single life.
Or immigrants who keep the tongue
   and customs of their mother
   country spliced within them
   in a newer world.
           Or why
   hereditary governments collapse
   when spliced with voters'
   rights.
           Or how belligerent
   stupidity spliced with neo-
   Hitlers blunders proudly
   into war.
           It's the saga of splice.
Once echoes twice.

The Fateful

The crash that killed him south
    of Lourmarin said more about
    absurdity than Albert Camus
    could put in books.
                   And so did
    Kennedy's indifference to danger.
Both men died unexpectedly
    by violence in ways that neither
    could expect.
                Why speculate?
Why not concede that anything
    can happen and leave it go
    at that?
            But facts persist.
They undermine us like the world's
    bad news that leaves us always
    in arrears.
            Poets assure us
    that everything's particular.
Philosophers bore and numb us
    with abstractions.
              A single
poem that reveals what hides
    behind a mask makes all
    philosophy the option of a fool.

True News

It's what we can't forget
    that lasts.
          It's why Elizabeth
remembers my brother
every year in January.
             It's how
    the female body in its prime
    attracts without pretense . . .
What's unforgettable reveals
    itself at will.
          Unlike
    mere memory, it happens
    when it must and never dims.
Seeing our very capitol
    mugged in session and mauled,
    we witnessed what defied denial.
What good did it do to wish
    a pox on mobs who smiled
    for show, strutted beneath
    flags, laughed without
    mirth, and raged for no
    reason?
          We'd seen it happen
    elsewhere before.
          It could
    happen again.
          Trying not
    to remember made us remember.

Conscientious Objection

You think you are killing me. I think you are
committing suicide.
—Antonio Porchia

Naming themselves as self-defenders
in chosen wars meant nothing.
While pacifiers waged to win
what pacifists worked to end,
the wars went on.
      After
they ended, some wondered why
they thought wars would ever be
different.
    As for peace?
No peace would linger longer
than the warriors allowed.
The wounded stayed wounded
for life.
    The rest returned
to lives no longer theirs.
Who mentions or explains why
veterans who chose to die
by choice exceeded sixty
thousand every year
for a decade?
      Their obituaries
were the same for a decade
previous.
    The only difference
was a date, a year, a name.

The Armored Man

Arma virumque cano
                              —Virgil

Toppled from armored horses,
    armored knights were defenseless.
Foot soldiers hacked them to death.
When armor took the form of tanks,
    the tactics of attackers were the same.
Crews trapped in crippled tanks
    huddled like targets in waiting.
God, how nothing has changed!
Nobody doubted that Hector's
    armor was sure to deflect
    the spear of Achilles.
                              Outflanked,
    the Maginot Line collapsed,
    and so fell France.
                         Penetrators
    won the Battle of the Bulge.
Offense, defense, struggle,
    outcome . . .
                     Bombardment now
can rid the world of Washington,
Boston, New York, Moscow,
and all that's left of Russia
in thirty minutes.
                      With no
deterrent but retaliation
fed by fear of extinction,
both sides can attack with force.

Defense will be irrelevant.
Armor will be irrelevant.
Defeat will be foreseen and mutual.

For Those Whose Names Are Titles

Look at them.
                    Given status
    by gender, age, and heredity,
    they're like performers in a play
    of their own making.
                    Distanced
    by centuries from all the numbered
    Henries, they have no exiles,
    plots, or executions to explain.
Their weddings and funerals
    are public holidays.
                    They're little
    more than royal bourgeoisie
    on show to lure the crowds.
Their counterparts are gone.
Each of the sixteen Louises
    of France had power plus wealth.
Napoleon put an end to that.
The Russian Revolution toppled
    the czars.
                    No Romanov survived.
When power bonds with blood,
    the options for revolt are unforeseen.
The founder of Saudi Arabia
    fathered forty-five sons
    to keep the country in his name.
Though he believed his legacy
    would thrive on brotherhood, he left
    a tyranny ruled by sperm.

Twin-Faced

Hypocrite lecteur!—mon semblable,—mon frere.
—Charles Baudelaire

Frowning, the frowner's not thinking
  but planning—planning.
                           He
  keeps his distance until
  he makes you think you need
  his help.
             Some women offer
  true smiles only to men
  of possible interest.
                  The President
tells his followers, "I love you."
Some kneel, some pray, some spit.
An oldster pretends he's dying
  to see if strangers will pause
  long enough to listen.
                  All those
  who weep the shrewdest at a wake
  are seeking notice or mention.
Attractive women seldom wed
  because they think they should.
Plotters pretend they're talking
  only to you—*just* you.
A well-to-do widow shared
  a lockbox with her spinster
  sister.
          After the widow died,
  the sister skipped the funeral,

emptied the lockbox, and flew
first class around the world.
Deceit and flattery will ravage
like assault and battery but not
by violence.
                        Everything near
will disappear as if by theft.
Of all that once was dear
and chosen, nothing will be left.

Time Told

1

It's four in the morning.
                 I wake
    and wait for something to happen.
When nothing happens, I assume
    that nothing will.
               I find
    myself trying to remember
    all I've forgotten while forgetting
    what I should remember.
Yesterday pretends it's tomorrow
    although it's still today.

2

Centered on screen, a newscaster
    passes on what passes for
    the passing distraction of news.
Since time kills news the minute
    it's born, I'm watching a funeral.

3

He had the window seat.
After takeoff he told me,
    "My line is shoes; what's yours?"
I said I was a writer.
He smiled the smile of the least
    impressed.

"What do you write?"
"I never know in advance."
"Where
are you headed now?"
I told him
I'd been invited to recite
my poems at a university.
"They pay you for that?"

4

If ahead is where we are rowing,
and behind is where we have gone,
we face wherever we've gone
with our backs to wherever we're going.

Stratford Is Anywhere

> Poetry should be read as carefully as menus
> in expensive restaurants.
>
> —Adam Zagajewski

What Shakespeare means to Stratford
    matches what Seferis means
    to Greece, Goethe to Germany,
    Yeats and Heaney to the Irish,
    and Lorca to Spain.
                        What
    makes us care where poets lived
    or died?
            If poets live only
    when they're read or heard,
    biography is just a footnote.
Asked once by a scholar where
    Edgar Allan Poe lived
    in Baltimore, a city official
    said the house had been replaced
    by a foreign car dealership.
Where's the poetry in that?

Steps and Stones

Her black hair is cut short
  and parted on the right.
              She's
  dancing near the Parthenon
  with two men on either side
  of her, their hands aligned
  on one another's shoulders.
Her feet are speaking fluently
  in Greek.
              Bouzoukis match
  her every step . . .
              In fact,
  she's dancing on what's left
  of the Acropolis—a cemetery
  now of crumbled stones
  that sleep with history and other
  lies.
              Concluding the sirtaki,
  the dancers smile and wave.
The stones foreshadow oldness
  without end.
              The dancers
  disagree.
              They make their own
  tempo, and there's no debris.

Sledding

He wakes to what he calls
    fast snow.
                It gleams like ice . . .
Prone on his sled, he speeds
    unchecked until the sled
    assumes complete control.
Unable to steer or stop,
    he feels possessed by a wild
    recklessness that stifles
    fear in all its flavors.
What's safe or dangerous is
    unforeseeably ahead.
If safe, he'll credit God,
    coincidence, or luck.
If not, he'll blame the sled.

All the Difference

Catholic churches close
    or conjoin like grocery stores
    with dwindling customers.
                        Bishops
    blame disbelief and close more . . .
Reactions to presidents who lie
    differ.
              One president
    barely ducked a thrown shoe
    at a press briefing in Iraq.
A more fluent president
    was excused because "he wore
    a suit well . . ."
              In advertisements
    for beer or shaving lotion,
    retired quarterbacks shift
    from gridirons to television spots . . .
For saying the same things,
    men and women utter
    different verbs.
               Men look,
    choose, buy, assume,
    fret, forget, demand,
    shout, and tip.
             Women
    notice, consider, shop,
    suppose, wait, remind,
    request, whisper, and thank.

High, Higher, Highest

Viewed from space, the world's
   impersonal.
                  France appears,
   but no Frenchmen.
                  Then Germany,
   without one German.
                  Regardless,
the richest man on earth
pays three hundred thousand
for a ten-minute flight by rocket
at three thousand miles per hour
to see everything below
from sixty-two miles straight up.
He's making business plans
   for space, beginning with Mars
   and the moon.
                  There's ample
precedent to prove how profit
motivates.
                  After we mapped
the earth as we imagined it,
we matched what we imagined
with the world as it would look
when photographed from space.
We did the same with rivers,
   lakes, and seas.
                  We kept
the original names unchanged
for everything we saw
as far as we could fly.

From seashores to the stratosphere,
    we saw the world as property
    that men could bargain for and buy.
We see it now the same
    while profiteers debate how best
    to advertise and sell the sky.

PART THREE

Alone with Presences

Paying my tax bill can wait.
Some huckster hawking condos
    in Belize can leave a message.
King Death can keep his terrors
    to himself for once.
                        I live
    by preference in space where clocks
    have no hands, and time
    is what it is when there is
    nothing else to think about.
Infinity takes over long enough
    for me to reunite with those
    I loved the most.
                    It eases me
    to feel they're near, which proves
    those gone are never gone.
I play backgammon with my father
    in a dream and lose and lose.
I'm talking Plato with my brother
    in Annapolis.
                    It's then and now
    where FDR and JFK stay
    quotably alive while Marilyn
    Monroe survives and thrives
    in all her blonde availability.
Are these as everlasting
    as my aunt's devotion or my mother's
    smile when she sang or how
    my brother faced his last
    Epiphany without a whimper?

Who says that those who've gone
        are ever out of sight or mind?
They're present but invisible.
                        They visit
        when they choose.
                        They rule the world.

Yes

Nora Barnacle preferred
    James Joyce the tenor
    to Joyce the writer.
                    She
    compared him to McCormick
    but thought his writings trivial.
Even after *Dubliners*
    appeared, they lived like paupers
    in Zurich, Trieste, and Paris.
One critic said, "In *Dubliners*
    Joyce never wrote better—
    just differently later."
                 If *later*
    meant *Ulysses*, he had
    a point.
          "You have to be
    from Dublin to understand *Ulysses*,"
    declared one Irishman.
He had a point as well.
After the publishing struggles,
    the smuggling of copies from Paris,
    the legal hassles, and the pirated
    editions, *Ulysses* found
    its place.
          Judged legally
    literary were nipples, scrotums,
    sphincters, and the grunts, squeals,
    and utterings of lovers coupling
    in the very act.

One wife's
unpunctuated ramble sold
more books than all the praise
combined of Eliot, Pound,
Fitzgerald, Faulkner, Hemingway,
and even Einstein.
Molly Bloom's
soliloquy attracted millions
and attracts them still.
Derived
from letters to an Irish tenor
from his wife, Molly's monologue
explains in fact just how
Ulysses happened and ended.
Joyce must have known
that Nora Barnacle, who loved
his voice but not his books,
would have the final word.

"Attention, Attention Must Finally Be Paid To Such A Person"

The title sounded like a tired
    headline without resonance—
    Death of a Salesman.
                        Nothing
    could stop me from going.
                        After
    walking twenty-seven blocks
    to the Morosco, I paid three dollars
    for a seat in the fourth-row center.
Behind me sat Charlie Spivak,
    whose trumpeting I knew.
                        Seconds
    before the lights dimmed,
    a tall man took an aisle seat
    in my very row.
                        It was
Arthur Miller come to watch
Lee J. Cobb, Mildred Dunnock,
Arthur Kennedy, Cameron
Mitchell, and (possibly) Dustin
Hoffman as young Bernard
create his play.
                        By the time
    it ended, I was changed.
                        Leaving,
I passed John Garfield
    in the lobby.
                        He seemed as moved
    as I was, but even more so.

Rewalking twenty-seven blocks
    to my hotel, I felt historical.
Later I would boast I'd seen
    the original (for me the only)
    cast.
                Once on a writers'
    panel chaired by Arthur Miller,
    I asked if Hoffman was
    the *first* Bernard.
                        He nodded.
But that seemed trivial
    beside the memory of such
    a play consummately designed
    (Mielziner), directed (Kazan),
    and staged.
                Over the years
    I witnessed Thomas Mitchell,
    Frederic March, an older
    Hoffman, and Brian Dennehy
    as Willie Loman, but none
    could rival Cobb and *the* cast.
Back at the hotel my father
    asked me the name of the play.
A salesman himself, he looked
    both disappointed and offended
    when he heard the humdrum title
    and wondered why I went.

Last Words

On the eve of July the first,
    Victoria announced, "We're
    running out of June."
Afterward, she laughed.
The laugh seemed more ironic
    than casual.
            It made me
    think that that could be
    a final line for each
    of us.
        "We're running out
of—."
        Fill in the month
    that fits.
        Forget the laugh.

A Newer Order

Biting his cigar, an Air Force
   general was bent on bombing
   Vietnam back to the Stone Age.
A war earlier, he'd firebombed
   Tokyo to ashes, human
   and otherwise.
                    Last week
   a Las Vegas billionaire
   demanded that Gaza be bombed
   back to the Stone Age.
                    Both men
   resembled one another: fat
   around the belly, frowningly
   serious, flanked by sycophants,
   and affluent.
                 Without four stars
   or a fortune fleeced from suckers
   at casino games, they'd be
   ignorable.
                Frankly, they sold
   the Stone Age short.
                   Aborigines
   learned to work with tools
   and fire, hunted animals
   instead of one another, housed
   their young in the safety of caves,
   and coped with dangers well
   enough to keep the race
   from vanishing.

Recently we've done
the opposite.
Historians confirm
we've killed more people in the last
half-century or so than any
nation now or ever, executed
thousands, and stocked the country
with more guns than people.
Currently we tally seventy
homicides per day compared
to thirty-five per year in Japan.
To match that kind of savagery
the Stone Age fails to qualify.
But who am I to talk?
While hundreds suffer and die
with our assent in Gaza, I watch
baseball on TV where millionaires
in uniform are playing a boy's game
to keep me shamefully distracted
from the world we say we're saving.

The Last Unfallen Leaf

No longer green, it's topped
    with tan and tipped with yellow.
In April it was one of millions.
In February snow, it stays
    a majority of one.
                    In a world
    that crowns longevity, it's king.
Younger, I'd be amused.
Older, I'm not sure now
    of being sure of anything.
Who wants to be the last
    surviving member of a family?
Or live marooned with all
    the fruit and coconuts you need
    but not a soul in sight?
Or waken as the mate still left
    to feel the living absence
    of the mate taken?
                    The questions
hurt.
        It's snowing harder.
I want the leaf to fall.

Missing the Missing

Old photographs do not console.
They mock.
                    They gladden sadly.
They resurrect the dead as well
    as those who look no longer
    as they looked.
                    For weeks I've sorted
    photographs from decades back:
    my aunt—father—brother—
    Albert my colleague—my neighbors
    Lynn and John—Harry
    the chancellor—and Grace of the ties
    and cufflinks.
                    Gone, they've taken
    back a self they brought
    to life in me each time
    we met.
                    Seeing them now
    in black and white and color
    makes it seem I've lost them
    twice.
                    Why am I doing this?
Photo after photo wounds me.
But still I look.
                    I miss them.
I miss the people we became
    when we sat down and talked.
I miss that.
                    I miss us.

Lottie

Her given name meant "gentle,"
    but everyone called her Lottie,
    except the nuns.
                    They thought
Lottie was short for Charlotte.
As Charlotte she taught, became
    a nurse, and spoke with ease
    in three languages.
               As Lottie
    she played the lute and sang
    to her own accompaniment and once
    with a pianist from the New York
    Philharmonic.
             After she chose
    my father, he ordered from Damascus
    a lute specifically sized
    for her.
          I still have it.
She cared enough to adopt
    a Serbian girl until
    her parents could immigrate.
In a one-line letter to my aunt,
    she wrote, "Hi, Sis, how's
      your love life?"
             She died
    when I was six.
             Decades back,
    a woman I'd never met
    stopped me and said, "I'm named
    after your mother."

                    She smiled
as if she'd kept a vow
she'd made to tell me that.

September Eleventh

Foreseeable or not, it made us
    wince the way that Kennedy's
    public murder made us wince.
We headed for home exactly
    as we did four decades back.
We sat like mutes before
    a screen and watched.
                        And watched.
Overnight, the President renamed
    America the "Homeland."
                        Travail
    and travel by air became
    one and the same.
                    Architects
    competed to design the ultimate
    memorial.
                Pulpit and public
    oratory droned like Muzak
    on demand.
                    Attempting to assuage,
    one mayor noted that three
    thousand victims numbered less
    than one month's highway deaths
    across the country . . .
                        But nothing
    could blur the filmed moment
    of impact, the slowly buckling
    floors and girders and glass,
    a blizzard of papers swirling
    in smoke, and finally two people

out of thirty-nine who chose
to jump instead of burn—a man
and woman, probably co-workers,
plummeting together hand
in hand from the hundredth floor
to ground zero at thirty-two
feet per second per second.

Afterthoughts in Advance

For the house you chose for us
    that still fits.
               For the cycled
flowers you planted to bloom
in different months all summer.
For showing me that feeling
    is always surer than thinking.
For telling me to dot my *i*'s.
For knowing what to ignore
    and how.
             For smiling truthfully
    in photographs.
             For letting
your heart make up your mind.
For not letting your heart
    make up your mind.
             For knowing
    the difference.
             For feeling the pain
of total strangers as your own.
For buying a drum for Sam.
For buying the second and third
    and then the piano.
             For saving
whatever becomes in time
more savable because you saved it.
For thinking of the dead as always
    present but unseen.
             For being
dear when near but dearer

when not.
    For laughing until
you have to sneeze.
        For knowing
that money is better to give
when alive than leave when dead.
For keeping spare dollars in your
    coat pockets just in case.
For proving that silence is truer
    than talk each time we touch
    or look into each other's eyes
    and hear the silence speak.

Suspended Sentence

A clean slice through the neck
    of a rooster separates the rooster's
    head from its body.
                Beheaded,
    the body runs in circles,
    flapping its wings until
    it realizes that it's dead
    already and dies for good.
Between the first and final
    death?
             Suspense.
                  Ted
    at ninety-five was asked
    how being ninety-five felt.
"I died ten years ago,"
    he said, "ask somebody else."
Told he had three months to live,
    Bronco demanded, "Which three?"
When one comic turned a hundred
    on his sick bed and was asked
    what words he wanted spoken
    at his funeral, he answered,
    "Surprise me."
               Other epitaphs
    survive, but none can match
    the secrecy of Lazarus.
               Apart
    from Christ, no one but Lazarus
    died and returned, and Lazarus

alone was doomed to face
death twice.
        The rooster in him
should have balked at such
a fate, unless he'd glimpsed
some preview of an afterlife
between deaths one and two
that silenced all his doubts.
Why did he keep that to himself?

Overtime

It's much too late to think
   of options or alternatives.
Our pharaoh-in-chief is waiting
   like a spoiled prince for loyalists
   to kiss his ring.
               Meanwhile
the little we have saved is taxed
for war.
        No one admits
we've made a hoax of peace
by living behind locked doors
and stashing dollars for the worst.
We're drunk with ultra-security,
   ultra-speed, ultra-vitamins,
   ultra-power.
           We converse
through machines.
             We think
in slogans.
          We worship glitz
and notoriety.
          We choose novels
for "easy reading."
          As for poetry?
It's all reduced to wordplay
and sociology.
         Meanwhile,
the televised and tattooed world
slides by disguised as normal.

We sit and watch.
                    Even
        when seated, we keep a pistol
        holstered at the hip and ready.

Galeano

Until lions have their own historians, histories of the
hunt will glorify the hunters.
          —African proverb

You earned what all great writers
    earn: derision, envy,
    prison, exile, hatred,
    and immortality.
               For courage
on a page, no one comes close
to you.
          Who else has shown
the world its "open veins"?
And who but you could call
    Neruda, Otero, and Alastair
    Reid his friends?
            I often
wish my Spanish was good
enough to read your books
in Spanish and see *exactamente*
what's lost in translation.
             First among
your enemies were slave owners,
killers, and torturers.
            While some
considered the body a sin,
a machine, or a business, you called
the body a fiesta.
          Soccer
alone deserved a book

from you and got it.
                    Balding,
you sought a cure, found none,
and lived thereafter boldly bald.
There's no replacing you.
                    Exiled
for years in Spain, you waited
for Uruguay to change.
                    Braulio
Lopez, a guitarist in Montevideo
who sang the anthems of rebellion,
had his fingers crushed in prison.
Deported, he shunned all talk
of his imprisonment when you
contacted him in Barcelona:
"My hands will heal, I'll play
and sing again, and I don't
want to doubt the applause."
Eduardo, even you could not
have spoken more nobly than that.

Venus

Consider Victorine Meurent
    in Manet's *Le Déjeuner sur l'herbe.*
She seems more naked than nude
    between two well-dressed men
    who stare past her while she
    looks straight at Manet—and us.
The Barcelona whores Picasso
    chose for *Les Demoiselles d'Avignon*
    appear less sensual than awkward.
Clothed or not, Goya's
    Maja looks bored.
                Pearlstein's
    nudes seem too tired to care . . .
But nudity for Venus looks
    permanent by preference.
The breasts of the girl from Milos
    that Alexandros chose to model
    are sculpted exactly to scale.
Two thousand years later
    in the same Aegean, his sculpture
    was discovered cracked in half
    with both arms missing.
                Reborn
    complete in polished marble,
    she's draped from the pubis down
    to show her torso upward
    from the hips without a flaw.
Turned a fraction to the left,
    she's stayed at ease alone

in the Louvre for two centuries
or more.
         There's not a sign
of Eve's remorse or any hint
of Christian shame or guilt.
This lady's nude and unembarrassed.
No one has matched her since.

P A R T   F O U R

We Live With Our Deceptions

September through December
        are numbered out of sequence . . .
Restrooms are not for resting . . .
To qualify as a founder, one
        of the Founding Fathers fathered
        a foundling . . .
                        Sudden death
        is the common enemy that soldiers
        of opposing armies face
        together.
                        All wars permit
        strangers to murder strangers
        legally . . .
                        Weak men belittle
        women because they fear them . . .
Women feel what they say
        and do.
                        A woman's smile
        is her handshake.
                        Teresa
        of Ávila danced flamenco
        in the convent.
                        Ordered by the Papal
        Nuncio to stop the practice,
        Teresa Ali Fatima Corella
        Sanchez de Cepeda y Ahumada
        slapped him in the face.
                        Four
        centuries later she was named
        the first female Doctor

of the Church . . .
                    Newspaper
headlines do not announce
or report the news but inflict it . . .
Football was "run, tackle
and block" until Rockne
featured the forward pass
to prove that throwing over
was smarter than running through . . .
Football and hockey live
and die by the clock . . .
                    The eyes
of a house are windows that become
polite when curtained . . .
                    Looking
upward instead of inward
silences the voice of God
within us . . .
                For bravery
in public?
            Jacqueline
Kennedy's four days in November.

Nightly

I wake each day to face
    the tyranny of certainties
    that rhyme with age.
                Next come
    the obstinate laws of science
    where life is only what
    I taste, touch, see, hear, or smell
    as well as what I name
    in passing with the wand of words.
For some who look for more,
    there's always the mythology
    of God's parting the Red Sea
    or Christ's walking on the waves
    of Galilee.
            As for the righteous
    who assume that miracles will spare
    them everything they fear?
I leave them to their dreams . . .
I trust in love ongoing
    from time present into presence.
I'm grateful for seven hundred
    and fifty-three months we shared
    and share still, share now.
                You
    made a poem out of each day's
    prose.
        To live that life
    again for one more day
    with you, I'd swap the world.

One Night at a Time

You kept the outcome at a distance
    with your smile, but the end
    was scripted in advance.
                        Each time
    our eyes locked, the tears
    came.
               I had to turn away.
You held my hand—the left.
Each night in what passes
    now for sleep, I wake
    to learn how absence crucifies.
What can I do to give
    this grief an ounce of dignity?
Nothing compares with it.
Only the ache of not having
    you beside me brings you
    back and keeps you close.

Stages

Lose parents, and you lose the past. Lose
children, and you lose the future. Lose your
mate, and you lose the present.
—An adage

Without having you to care
   or care for, I'm as helpless
   as a driver of a car sliding
   sideways downhill on ice,
I've lost my taste for all
   enjoyment.
                  Some say diversion
   is the answer.
                  I say diversion
   is distraction, nothing more.
Others say I should be
   grateful for the years we shared.
I say I am, *I am,*
   but what I feel is truer
   than words or years.
                        Because
   forever has no dates, I'm
   jealous of eternity and God.

One Year More, One Year Less

Without you I am sentenced
        to myself.
                The house we chose
together has a past that's always
present: Waterford glasses
you treasured, sunflowers
you brought from Cannes and vased,
the sculpture Starchev gave you
after you praised it.
                        They help me
        feel you're near.
                        In photographs
you smile as a bride, a wife,
and later as a mother hugging
three grandchildren on our sixtieth.
Never forced or false, your smile
        was everywhere and always
        you.
                Each day for more
        than sixty years that smile
        saved me.
                        And saves me still.

God's Gift to Me

My dearest Mary Anne,
    I'm no more reconciled
    than I was three months ago.
You're everywhere I look—
    from raincoats hangered
    in a closet—to framed photographs—
    to car keys for a car
    you never drove.
              I sleep
    and wake now on your side
    of the bed.
          To say that other
    men have lost their wives
    is no relief.
          Devastation
    stays particular and merciless
    if shared or not.
          Longevity
    offers nothing but more
    of the same or worse . . .
             I miss
    your face, your voice, your calm
    defiance in your final months,
    your last six words that will be
    mine alone forever.
You were my life as surely
    as you are my life today
    and will be always.
          We're close
    as ever now but differently.

"Why do we have to die?"
   you asked.
                  I had no answer.
My answer now is rage
   and tears that sentence death
   to death each day I wake
   without but always with you.

One Another's Best

It happens when what I say
  and what I'd hope to say
  are one and the same, and even
  better than I hoped.
                    The sure
  perfection of it lingers.
Gratitude seems not enough.
I want to let the world
  know, but quietly—so quietly
  that no one hears me but
  myself.
            It's like discovering
  love for the first, last,
  and only time.
                    The once
  of it gladdens but saddens.
"Sorrow ends," wrote Shakespeare,
  "not when it seemeth done."
My only one, my dearest,
  your requiem and birthday
  happened together.
                    Was this
  your way or God's of promising
  that right now and forever
  would someday be the same
  for us, regardless of the odds?

Once

If once means once, once twice
    is impossible.
                Once is quick
    as a struck match.
                  But once
    can be a song that keeps
    singing after it's sung.
Or a poem that's once and always
    at the same time.
                  To be complete
    it has to end, but once
    it's over, it begins again.

The Next Time We Saw Paris

"The next time was the last time."

One morning we saw de Gaulle
    himself in uniform chauffeured
    alone in an open Peugeot.
He seemed to dare assassination
    as he did near Notre Dame
    during the Liberation Parade.
On house fronts and doors we noticed
    small bronze plaques with names
    followed by *Victime de Nazis*.
We'd read reports that *Enfants*
    des Boches reached one hundred thousand
    during the Occupation.
                  "Horizontal
collaborators" were shorn bald,
    spat upon, and marched naked
    through the streets.
                De Gaulle
pronounced all executed traitors
    justly punished.
             Visitors
toured Paris of the postcards: Sacre
    Coeur and the Eiffel Tower.
The Folies-Bergere booked sellouts.
The Bateaux Mouches was packed.
Lounging by the Seine, a fisherman
    propped his rod against
    a bench and smoked a Gitanes
    as if catching a fish meant
    little or nothing at all.

Night in the Eye of the Sun

In La Napoule with Mary Anne
    I order mussels steamed
    with aioli, two cappuccinos,
    and a warm baguette with butter.
It's almost dusk in La Napoule.
Two waiters are laughing in French
    and folding serviettes.
                We talk
    of Avignon and Aix-en-Provence
    where thousands of sunflowers
    follow the sun to sleep,
    and aisles of lavender look
    truer than they are.
              We say
if colors can intoxicate, these do
and then some.
           It's darkening
in La Napoule.
         We dine
like partners who have earned
the ease that work makes possible
and doubly bountiful because
it's earned.
        Throughout America,
where ease means laziness,
that art is lost.
        In La Napoule
the night is ours to waste
creatively.

The buttered crust
of our baguette tastes almost
like the Eucharist.

Tomorrow, fireworks
will celebrate the fall of the Bastille
before the coast grows calm
again.

The docked and anchored
yachts will mute their lights.
Beach crews will stack the sunning
mats like so much stock.
The sea that hides more history
than all the oceans in the world
will slow its tides.

But that
is still a sun away.

Our private
table feels so much like home
that we forget the time.
It's midnight now in La Napoule.

A Love like No Other

It happens rarely, if at all.
Age means little.
                    History
          means less.
                    All that matters
          is the mystery.
                    From infancy
          to manhood our son's love
          for his godmother never lessened.
Sixty years between them
          made no difference.
                              For hours
          they could sit in the same room,
          say little or nothing and be
          perfectly happy.
                              Once
          she even let him cut
          her hair . . .
                              A decade later
          she told my wife during
          their last moments together,
          "A very nice young man
          always comes to see me,
          and he looks just like your son."

Saved from the Sea

Choppy or calm, the sea
    bothers me.
               It always seems
    to be lying in wait.
                    Always.
Before I was six, I fell
    unseen from a dock and was saved
    from drowning by a stranger.
That moment comes to me
    in dreams—the sinking, the saving.
Now I swim well enough
    to save myself, but doubts
    still bother me.
                I never
  relax in the water.
                  Never.
Even when I've dared myself
    to swim farther than I should
    and back, the sea still wins.
It never loses.
           It never
  will.
      It never can.

Worlds Apart

An American billionaire donates
    a miniature sub and flies
    expert engineers to Thailand
    to offer free expertise.
Divers from multiple nations
    volunteer their services
    to save twelve boys and their
    soccer coach trapped
    in a flooded cave for weeks.
Knowing their lives could be
    at risk, they dive regardless.
One dies, but the boys and coach
    are saved . . .
                Elsewhere?
                   Mothers
    stranded in Texas or Mexico
    weep for children sundered
    and lost—assassins gun down
    concertgoers or third graders
    with weapons of war—hundreds
    of refugees in flight from Libya
    drown near Sicily—Trumpism
    trumps Trump—Israeli
    snipers near Gaza target
    three unarmed boys
    protesting at the border, killing
    all three, their catch for the day.

Thou Shalt Kill

On D-Day alone, ten thousand
   died.
         Cemeteries in France
commemorate them, grave
by grave . . .
            The battle of Tarawa
lasted for seventy-two
hours.
         One thousand
Marines were killed or drowned.
Their bodies floated facedown
   in the tide or sprawled half-buried
   in the sand.
            Of four thousand
eight hundred Japanese,
only seventeen survived . . .
Nations rightly honor
   the lost.
         But killing is killing.
When waged for honor and other
   deceits, war makes the killing
   likelier and lawful . . .
            Historians
claim that Greece made war
on Troy over a kidnapped wife
   named Helen.
         In fact, Helen
welcomed the abduction.

                    Paris
was young and handsome compared
with the braggart she married.

                              Greeks
would fight to save a kidnapped
wife, but not one who loved
her abductor.

                    They settled instead
for a plausible lie.

                    Determined
to trade on the Black Sea
that Troy controlled, the Greeks
knew war was the key but only
if seen as noble.

                    Rescuing
Helen of Troy from Troy
is what their cause became . . .
When dangers widen into wars,
    what worked at Troy has worked
    the same in all wars since
    though Troy is off the map,
    and Helen has changed her name.

            For Stuart Herrington

Vengeance

Married and titled as Lady
    Caroline Lamb, she was twice
    a mother.
               Byron was Lord
Byron, whose hobby was women.
"Mad, bad, and dangerous to know,"
    she said of him.
             "No love
    could be outdone," she added,
    "like one that's felt for the first
    time."
           Their bond was poetry
    and passion.
          To meet him
    in secret she dressed as a boy
    or wore a mask.
           Knowing
    he was clubfooted, she flirted
    and danced with total strangers
    while he watched.
            Not once but twice
    she fought him with a knife before
    she was subdued.
          Repeated
    spats defined them as a pair.
After they spat their last,
    she mailed what she believed
    was all he understood of love—
    two snippets of her pubic hair.

Weddings These Days

1

The bride came to church on a tractor.
The groom and groomsmen
    were filmed helping her board.
The tractor itself resembled
    a semi-tank on treads.
The groom did all the driving
    while his bride sat beside him
    and frowned.
                What everybody
    would always remember
    would be farm machinery driven
    by a groom with more nerve
    than taste.
              The bride never smiled.
Dressed in virginal white
    and wielding a bouquet (since this
    was, after all, *her* wedding), she thought
    this whole charade would vanish
    if she just sat still . . .
              It stayed.

2

One bride at her wedding chomped on
    loud bubble gum while flouncing
    down the aisle.
             At another,
    the groom wore high-laced

yellow sneakers.
                         At a third,
the bride dallied for an hour
outside the church because
she wanted to be sure.
                         At a fourth
were two who took each other
for better or worse while skydiving
down to Texas.
                         Another two
exchanged self-written vows
with sign language side by side
in divers' apparatus underwater.
The sixth and last was a home
     wedding where the groom,
     having fainted twice, was married
     seated, determined but incoherent.

Helen of Duke

We never met.
                    I knew you
only through a book you mailed
to me inscribed.
                    You wrote
you married Bevington "just once . . .
forever."
                    *A Book and a Love
Affair* tells what that meant.
I learned you read to him
     (at *his* request) in hospice.
Afterward, you traveled:
     Spain, England, Crete, Kenya,
     France, Tibet, Egypt,
     Brazil, Peru.
                    You published
     travel diaries that read
     like Augustine's *Confessions*.
After your crippled son
     chose suicide, you traveled
     even more.
                    You came to know
     MacLeish by watching his eyes
     when he spoke, pronounced Reagan's
     optimism nothing but an act,
     and joked with cummings over drinks.
When William Carlos Williams
     told you that girls found him
     handsomer at sixty than he was

at twenty, you said, "Do you
want to bet?"
              The chore of travel
lessened to a bore.
                  You ran out
of destinations.
              You found
television a two-dimensional
fake of a three-dimensional
world.
          It lost in depth
what it gained in length and width.
After your mother died,
you wrote, "A better life
is better than death."
                  Time
past returned as time present,
and your longest journey became
the distance from midnight to morning.

The Fate of Nothing

The Devil's first trick is his Incognito.
—Denis de Rougemont

Forget the pitchfork, the red
    pajamas, and the Satan sideshow.
Save those for Halloween.
What's diabolical reflects
    deficiency.
              When we lack
courage, the lack is devilish.
If we lack love and let it
    molder into hate, the lack
    is devilish.
              When Omar Khayyam
said, "I myself am heaven
and hell," he meant that God
and fate existed within him.
It's always been like that.
If we resist, we keep
    hell at bay.
              If we
succumb, the devil has
his way with us.
              In case
you've forgotten, the word *evil*
hides within the word
devil.
              It's more than symbolic.
It's literally true and shows
    what's mocked us since the world

began.
           Where some see losses,
   others see gains.
               Where others
  see pleasure, some see pain.
No matter what we see or do,
   we're never certain in advance
   if what we do is right,
   or what we see is true.
What else explains why Abel
   noticed nothing in his brother
   to suggest his killer would be Cain?
By then it was too late
   for anything but hate.
               And fate.

By Chance

It seems too minor to mention—
    the day a Frenchman found
    my car keys in Provence and refused
    a tip.
           "*Pour la France*," he said
    and smiled . . .
                 Or how my son
    at seven braved the bees
    to bring me Windex to defend
    myself against them.
                    My thanks?
"Get back inside right now . . ."
Or Monk, who saved his nephew's
    life by giving him his kidney.
"I just need one," he said . . .
Or how Mary's adopted
    daughter from St. Petersburg
    starred in high school soccer
    and never talked of Russia . . .
What happens without notice
    or acclaim reminds me how
    a ship that's spotted by a man
    marooned for years but saved
    can almost civilize the sea.

The Renegade

As for life after death?
              Many
      believe, but no one really
      knows.
                    All those who claim
      they know equate belief
      with knowledge for psychiatric,
      not spiritual, reasons.
                          They
      find living with uncertainty
      impossible.
                    Believers pray
      in gratitude, but doubts persist
      even with the most devout.
They want to take Christ's words
      as scrivened by his four
      stenographers and say amen.
Death is the problem—the fact
      of death.
                    Reactions range
      from fear to love.
                          The fearful
      die living.
                    Even when those
      most loved are taken, lovers
      discover that love buries death.
The dead survive as presences
      in dreams or thoughts that mock
      whatever passes for eternal
      rest.

After thirty-three
years of breath and three days
of death, the Savior rose
to resume living with those
He loved.
Compared to that,
who needs theology or ritual
for reassurance?
What's truer for God
or each of us than unions
resurrected as reunions?
What else
is faith but hoping that loves
once known will be known forever?

The Odds

We want what's intimate to last
    as surely as we want the life
    of touch, taste, sight, scent, and sound
    to last forever.
                "Tomorrow
I'll be here no longer," Nostradamus
    whispered when he died.
Fontenelle near death described
    his fear "as nothing more
    than trying to go on living."
Dying of fever, Hopkins
    repeated, "I am so happy."
Reactions differ.
                Beliefs
belie believers.
                All
    that lasts are chosen loves
    and what we hope is hope
    to wage against uncertainty.

P A R T   F I V E

Now Is Next

While most religions prophesy
    what's next as paradise, eternity,
    heaven, and similar dreams,
    I think what's next should be
    a chosen love that's shared
    in perpetuity.
                Based on what
    I've seen and heard, all those
    who love and are loved in return
    pay little if any attention
    to statutes of limitation.
Love and love-in-waiting
    rhyme daily and beyond
    because each one reflects
    the other.
                Taken together,
    they make a fool of time.

The author of books of poetry, fiction, essays, and plays, **Samuel Hazo** is the founder and director of the International Poetry Forum in Pittsburgh, Pennsylvania. He is also McAnulty Distinguished Professor of English Emeritus at Duquesne University, where he taught for forty-three years. From 1950 until 1957 he served in the US Marine Corps, completing his tour as a captain. He earned his BA from the University of Notre Dame, his MA from Duquesne University, and his PhD from the University of Pittsburgh. Some of his previous works include *The Next Time We Saw Paris, And the Time Is*, and *Like a Man Gone Mad* (poetry); *The Time Remaining* and *If Nobody Calls, I'm Not Home* (fiction); *Tell It to the Marines* (drama); *The Stroke of a Pen, Outspokenly Yours, Smithereened Apart, The Pittsburgh That Stays within You*, and *The World within the Word: Maritain and the Poet* (essays). His translations include Denis de Rougemont's *The Growl of Deeper Waters*, Nadia Tueni's *Lebanon: Twenty Poems for One Love*, and Adonis's *The Pages of Day and Night*. In 2003 a selective collection of his poems, *Just Once*, received the Maurice English Poetry Award. A National Book Award finalist, he was named Pennsylvania's first state poet by Governor Robert Casey in 1993, and he served until 2003.